Eagle

A Force of Nature
Vision • Courage • Freedom

DayDreams Studio Press

"Totem Within Series"

This Book Belongs To:

_____

_____

Welcome,
Seeker of Vision

You Are A Force of Nature

————◆————

You hold in your hands
more than a journal—
you hold a sacred space
for transformation. Like
the eagle soaring above
the landscape, you are
invited to rise above the
ordinary and see your
life from a higher
perspective.

The Power of the Eagle

The eagle is seen as a symbol of enlightenment and rebirth, guiding those it chooses toward achieving greater heights and understanding. It encourages embracing challenges with courage and determination, with complete focus. This majestic bird also signifies the importance of viewing situations from a higher perspective.

The Eagle Symbolizes:

Vision -
Seeing clearly what others cannot

Courage -
Facing challenges with unwavering strength

Freedom -
Breaking free from limitations

Wisdom -
Understanding gained from soaring high

Renewal -
The capacity to reinvent and rejuvenate oneself.

As you write in this journal, embrace these qualities...

This is YOUR sacred space.
There are no rules, only invitations.

"You cannot fly like an eagle with the wings of a wren"
-William Henry Hudson's

_____

_____

_____

_____

_____

_____

_____

_____

_____

_____

_____

"In order to carry a positive action
we must develop here a positive vision" –
Dalai Lama

The keen vision of an eagle is a potent metaphor
for clearly identifying and focusing on a goal.

_____

_____

_____

_____

_____

_____

_____

_____

_____

_____

_____

Like a fledgling eagle taking its inaugural flight,
it takes belief and bravery to confront new
challenges in the face of fear.

_____

_____

_____

_____

_____

_____

_____

_____

_____

_____

_____

_____

_____

_____

_____

_____

_____

_____

_____

_____

_____

_____

_____

"No one outside ourselves can rule us inwardly.
When we know this, we become free." —
Buddha

_____

_____

_____

_____

_____

_____

_____

_____

_____

_____

_____

"We are not limited by what we have come to know—it is our openness to learn about ourselves that allows us to live fully."-JHS

_____

_____

_____

_____

_____

_____

_____

_____

_____

_____

_____

Reflecting
Consider what brings you joy:
The passions that flourish within you, and the
stories you could tell endlessly.

Stop to Discover *Ikigai* The Joy of a Meaningful Life Explore the intersection of your passions, skills, and purpose—much like a personal totem—to lead a more fulfilling life. This alignment will assist you in establishing goals that promote both personal and professional growth.

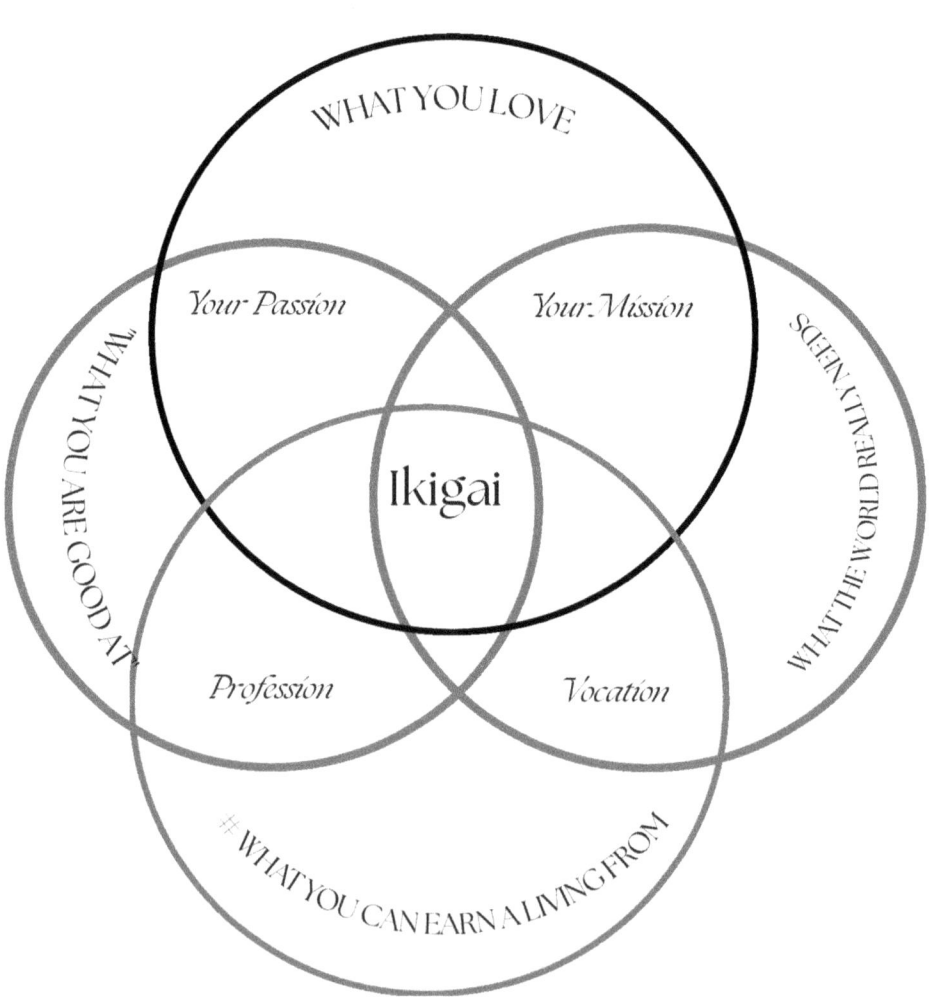

"In the journey of life, seek what lifts
your spirit and makes time stand still."

_____

_____

_____

_____

_____

_____

_____

_____

_____

_____

"Remember what you loved to do and who you were before the world told you who to be."

_____

_____

_____

_____

_____

_____

_____

_____

_____

_____

Like the eagle, you are meant to rise higher,
proving storms are not obstacles but steps
into strength."

_____

_____

_____

_____

_____

_____

_____

_____

_____

_____

To be born again is not to become
somebody else, but to become
ourselves." — Thomas Merton.

_____

_____

_____

_____

_____

_____

_____

_____

_____

_____

_____

"The eagle does not follow; it leads with strength and intention."

_____

_____

_____

_____

_____

_____

_____

_____

_____

_____

_____

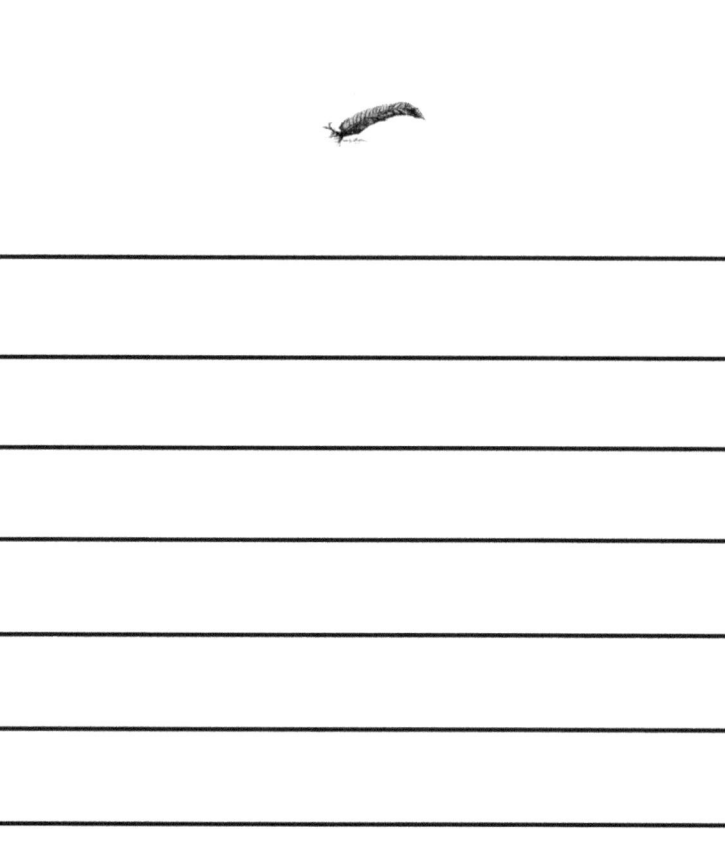

Eagles inspire with their graceful leadership and courage,
guiding us with wisdom from nature's heart.

_____

_____

_____

_____

_____

_____

_____

_____

_____

_____

"Journal writing is a voyage to the interior."
— Christina Baldwin

_____

_____

_____

_____

_____

_____

_____

_____

_____

_____

_____

_____

_____

_____

_____

_____

_____

_____

_____

_____

_____

_____

The Eagle has landed
- Neil Armstrong

What an amazing journey it is to
be one with the Eagle!

Final Thought

This journal represents
your dedication to
personal growth.

As you revisit these
pages, take a moment to
reflect on your journey
—observe how much you
have accomplished.

The eagle's flight is
everlasting—just like
your own journey.

May you have a beautiful life

Uncover your next totem animal!
Subscribe for updates, and enter for a
chance to win a complimentary journal at
https://joannesullam.com

www.ingramcontent.com/pod-product-compliance
Lightning Source LLC
Chambersburg PA
CBHW051633120626
46551CB00014B/2066